Enfranchisement Of Women: Reprinted From The "westminster Review" For July 1851...

Stuart Mill

Nabu Public Domain Reprints:

You are holding a reproduction of an original work published before 1923 that is in the public domain in the United States of America, and possibly other countries. You may freely copy and distribute this work as no entity (individual or corporate) has a copyright on the body of the work. This book may contain prior copyright references, and library stamps (as most of these works were scanned from library copies). These have been scanned and retained as part of the historical artifact.

This book may have occasional imperfections such as missing or blurred pages, poor pictures, errant marks, etc. that were either part of the original artifact, or were introduced by the scanning process. We believe this work is culturally important, and despite the imperfections, have elected to bring it back into print as part of our continuing commitment to the preservation of printed works worldwide. We appreciate your understanding of the imperfections in the preservation process, and hope you enjoy this valuable book.

London Borough of Enfield	
91200000519690	
Askews & Holts	Jul-2015
	£12.99

A general and four special committees were nominated, for the purpose of carrying on the undertaking until the next annual meeting.

According to the report in the 'New York Tribune,' above a thousand persons were present throughout, and "if a larger place could have been had, many thousands more would have attended." The place was described as "crowded from the beginning with attentive and interested listeners." In regard to the quality of the speaking, the proceedings bear an advantageous comparison with those of any popular movement with which we are acquainted, either in this country or in America. Very rarely in the oratory of public meetings is the part of verbiage and declamation so small, that of calm good sense and reason so considerable. The result of the Convention was in every respect encouraging to those by whom it was summoned: and it is probably destined to inaugurate one of the most important of the movements towards political and social reform, which are the best characteristic of the present age.

That the promoters of this new agitation take their stand on principles, and do not fear to declare these in their widest extent, without time-serving or compromise, will be seen from the resolutions adopted by the Convention, part of which we transcribe:—

"*Resolved*—That every human being, of full age, and resident for a proper length of time on the soil of the nation, who is required to obey the law, is entitled to a voice in its enactment; that every such person, whose property or labour is taxed for the support of the government, is entitled to a direct share in such government; therefore,

"*Resolved*—That women are entitled to the right of suffrage, and to be considered eligible to office, ... and that every party which claims to represent the humanity, the civilization, and the progress of the age, is bound to inscribe on its banners, equality before the law, without distinction of sex or colour.

"*Resolved*—That civil and political rights acknowledge no sex, and therefore the word 'male' should be struck from every State Constitution.

"*Resolved*—That, since the prospect of honourable and useful employment in after life is the best stimulus to the use of educational advantages, and since the best education is that we give ourselves, in the struggles, employments, and discipline of life; therefore it is impossible that women should make full use of the instruction already accorded to them, or that their career should do justice to their faculties, until the avenues to the various civil and professional employments are thrown open to them.

"*Resolved*—That every effort to educate women, without according to them their rights, and arousing their conscience by the weight of their responsibilities, is futile, and a waste of labour.

"*Resolved*—That the laws of property, as affecting married persons, demand a thorough revisal, so that all rights be equal between them; that the wife have, during life, an equal control over the property gained by their mutual toil and sacrifices, and be heir to her husband precisely to that extent that he is heir to her, and entitled at her death to dispose by will of the same share of the joint property as he is."

The following is a brief summary of the principal demands :—

"1. *Education* in primary and high schools, universities, medical, legal, and theological institutions.

"2. *Partnership* in the labours and gains, risks and remunerations of productive industry.

"3. *A coequal share* in the formation and administration of laws—municipal, State, and national—through legislative assemblies, courts, and executive offices."

It would be difficult to put so much true, just, and reasonable meaning into a style so little calculated to recommend it as the style of some of the resolutions. But whatever objection may be made to some of the expressions, none, in our opinion, can be made to the demands themselves. As a question of justice, the case seems to us too clear for dispute. As one of expediency, the more thoroughly it is examined the stronger it will appear.

That women have as good a claim as men have, in point of personal right, to the suffrage, or to a place in the jury-box, it would be difficult for any one to deny. It cannot certainly be denied by the United States of America, as a people or as a community. Their democratic institutions rest avowedly on the inherent right of every one to a voice in the government. Their Declaration of Independence, framed by the men who are still their great constitutional authorities—that document which has been from the first, and is now, the acknowledged basis of their polity, commences with this express statement:—

"We hold these truths to be self-evident: that all men are created equal; that they are endowed by their Creator with certain inalienable rights; that among these are life, liberty, and the pursuit of happiness; that to secure these rights, governments are instituted among men, deriving their just powers from the consent of the governed."

We do not imagine that any American democrat will evade the force of these expressions by the dishonest or ignorant subterfuge, that "men," in this memorable document, does not stand for human beings, but for one sex only; that "life, liberty, and the pursuit of happiness" are "inalienable rights" of only one moiety of the human species; and that "the governed," whose consent is affirmed to be the only source of just power, are meant for that half of mankind only, who, in relation to the other, have hitherto assumed the character of *governors*. The contradiction between principle and practice cannot be explained away. A like dereliction of the fundamental maxims of their political creed has been committed by the Americans in the flagrant instance of the negroes; of this they are learning to recognize the turpitude. After a struggle which, by many of its incidents, deserves the name of heroic, the abolitionists are now so strong in numbers and in influence that they hold the balance of parties in the United States. It was fitting that the men whose names will remain associated with the extirpation, from the democratic soil of America, of the aristocracy of colour, should be among the originators, for America and for the rest of the world, of the first collective protest against the aristocracy of sex; a distinction as accidental as that of colour, and fully as irrelevant to all questions of government.

Not only to the democracy of America, the claim of women to civil and political equality makes an irresistible appeal, but also to those radicals and chartists in the British Islands, and democrats on the Continent, who claim what is called universal suffrage as an inherent right, unjustly and oppressively withheld from them. For with what truth or rationality could the suffrage be termed universal, while half the human species remain excluded from it? To declare that a voice in the government is the right of all, and demand it only for a part—the part, namely, to which the claimant himself belongs—is to renounce even the appearance of principle. The chartist who denies the suffrage to women, is a chartist only because he is not a lord; he is one of those levellers who would level only down to themselves.

Even those who do not look upon a voice in the government as a matter of personal right, nor profess principles which require that it should be extended to all, have usually traditional maxims of political justice with which it is impossible to reconcile the exclusion of all women from the common rights of citizenship. It is an axiom of English freedom that taxation and representation should be co-extensive. Even under the laws which give the wife's property to the husband, there are many unmarried women who pay taxes. It is one of the fundamental doctrines of the British constitution, that all persons should be tried by their peers; yet women, whenever tried, are tried by male judges and a male jury. To foreigners the law accords the privilege of claiming that half the jury should be composed of themselves; not so to women. Apart from maxims of detail, which represent local and national rather than universal ideas, it is an acknowledged dictate of justice to make no degrading distinctions without necessity. In all things the presumption ought to be on the side of equality. A reason must be given why anything should be permitted to one person and interdicted to another. But when that which is interdicted includes nearly everything which those to whom it is permitted most prize, and to be deprived of which they feel to be most insulting; when not only political liberty but personal freedom of action is the prerogative of a caste; when even in the exercise of industry, almost all employments which task the higher faculties in an important field, which lead to distinction, riches, or even pecuniary independence, are fenced round as the exclusive domain of the predominant section, scarcely any doors being left open to the dependent class, except such as all who can enter elsewhere disdainfully pass by,—the miserable expediencies which are advanced as excuses for so grossly partial a dispensation, would not be sufficient, even if they were real, to render it other than a flagrant injustice. While, far from being expedient, we are firmly convinced that the division of mankind into two castes, one born to rule over the other, is in this case, as in all cases, an unqualified mischief; a source of perversion and demoralization, both to the favoured class and to those at whose expense they are favoured; producing none of the good which it is the custom to ascribe to it, and forming a bar, almost insuperable while it lasts, to any really vital improvement, either in the character or in the social condition of the human race.

These propositions it is now our purpose to maintain. But before entering on them, we would endeavour to dispel the preliminary objections which, in the minds of persons to whom the subject is new, are apt to prevent a real and conscientious examination of it. The chief of these obstacles is that most formidable one, custom. Women never have had equal rights with men. The claim in their behalf, of the common rights of mankind, is looked upon as barred by universal practice. This strongest of prejudices, the prejudice against what is new and unknown, has, indeed, in an age of changes like the present, lost much of its force; if it had not, there would be little hope of prevailing against it. Over three-fourths of the habitable world, even at this day, the answer, "It has always been so," closes all discussion. But it is the boast of modern Europeans, and of their American kindred, that they know and do many things which their forefathers neither knew nor did; and it is perhaps the most unquestionable point of superiority in the present above former ages, that habit is not now the tyrant it formerly was over opinions and modes of action, and that the worship of custom is a declining idolatry. An uncustomary thought, on a subject which touches the greater interests of life, still startles when first presented; but if it can be kept before the mind until the impression of strangeness wears off, it obtains a hearing, and as rational a consideration as the intellect of the hearer is accustomed to bestow on any other subject.

In the present case, the prejudice of custom is doubtless on the unjust side. Great thinkers, indeed, at different times, from Plato to Condorcet, besides some of the most eminent names of the present age, have made emphatic protests in favour of the equality of women. And there have been voluntary societies, religious or secular, of which the Society of Friends is the most known, by whom that principle was recognized. But there has been no political community or nation in which, by law and usage, women have not been in a state of political and civil inferiority. In the ancient world the same fact was alleged, with equal truth, in behalf of slavery. It might have been alleged in favour of the mitigated form of slavery, serfdom, all through the middle ages. It was urged against freedom of industry, freedom of conscience, freedom of the press; none of these liberties were thought compatible with a well-ordered State, until they had proved their possibility by actually existing as facts. That an institution or a practice is customary is no presumption of its goodness, when any other sufficient cause can be assigned for its existence. There is no difficulty in understanding why the subjection of women has been a custom. No other explanation is needed than physical force.

That those who were physically weaker should have been made legally inferior, is quite conformable to the mode in which the world has been governed. Until very lately, the rule of physical strength was the general law of human affairs. Throughout history, the nations, races, classes, which found themselves the strongest, either in muscles, in riches, or in military discipline, have conquered and held in subjection the rest. If, even in the most improved nations, the law of the sword is at last discountenanced as unworthy, it is only since the calumniated eighteenth century. Wars of conquest have only ceased since democratic revolutions began. The world is very young, and has but just begun to cast off injustice. It is only now getting rid of negro slavery. It is only now getting rid of monarchical despotism. It is only now getting rid of hereditary feudal nobility. It is only now getting rid of disabilities on the ground of religion. It is only beginning to treat men as citizens, except the rich and a favoured portion of the middle class. Can we wonder that it has not yet done as much for women? As society was constituted until the last few generations, inequality was its very basis; association grounded on equal rights scarcely existed; to be equals was to be enemies; two persons could hardly co-operate in anything, or meet in any amicable relation, without the law's appointing that one of them should be the superior of the other. Mankind have outgrown this state, and all things now tend to substitute, as the general principle of human relations, a just equality, instead of the dominion of the strongest. But of all relations, that between men and women being the nearest and most intimate, and connected with the greatest number of strong emotions, was sure to be the last to throw off the old rule and receive the new: for in proportion to the strength of a feeling, is the tenacity with which it clings to the forms and circumstances with which it has even accidentally become associated.

When a prejudice, which has any hold on the feelings, finds itself reduced to the unpleasant necessity of assigning reasons, it thinks it has done enough when it has re-asserted the very point in dispute, in phrases which appeal to the pre-existing feeling. Thus, many persons think they have sufficiently justified the restrictions on women's field of action, when they have said that the pursuits from which women are excluded are *unfeminine*, and that the *proper sphere* of women is not politics or publicity, but private and domestic life.

We deny the right of any portion of the species to decide for another portion, or any individual for another individual, what is and what is not their " proper sphere." The proper sphere for all human beings is the largest and highest which they are able to attain to. What this is, cannot be ascertained without complete liberty of choice. The speakers at the Convention in America have therefore done wisely and right, in refusing to entertain the question of the peculiar aptitudes either of women or of men, or the limits within which this or that occupation may be supposed to be more adapted to the one or to the other. They justly maintain, that these questions can only be satisfactorily answered by perfect freedom. Let every occupation be open to all, without favour or discouragement to any, and employments will fall into the hands of those men or women who are found by experience to be most capable of worthily exercising them. There need be no fear that women will take out of the hands of men any occupation which men perform better than they. Each individual will prove his or her capacities, in the only way in which capacities can be proved—by trial; and the world will have the benefit of the best faculties of all its inhabitants. But to interfere beforehand by an arbitrary limit, and declare that whatever be the genius, talent, energy, or force of mind of an individual of a certain sex or class, those faculties shall not be exerted, or shall be exerted only in some few of the many modes in which others are permitted to use theirs, is not only an injustice to the individual, and a detriment to society, which loses what it can ill spare, but is also the most effectual mode of providing that, in the sex or class so fettered, the qualities which are not permitted to be exercised shall not exist.

We shall follow the very proper example of the Convention, in not entering into the question of the alleged differences in physical or mental qualities between the sexes; not because we have nothing to say, but because we have too much; to discuss this one point tolerably would need all the space we have to bestow on the entire subject.* But if those who assert that the "proper sphere" for women is the domestic, mean by this that they have not shown themselves qualified for any other, the assertion evinces great ignorance of life and of history. Women have shown fitness for the highest social functions, exactly in proportion as they have been admitted to them. By a curious anomaly, though ineligible to even the lowest offices of State, they are in some countries admitted to the highest of all, the regal; and if there is any one function for which they have shown a decided vocation, it is that of reigning. Not to go back to ancient history, we look in vain for abler or firmer rulers than Elizabeth; than Isabella of Castile; than Maria Theresa; than Catherine of Russia; than Blanche, mother of Louis IX. of France; than Jeanne d'Albret, mother of Henri Quatre. There are few kings on record who contended with more difficult circumstances, or overcame them more triumphantly, than most of these. Even in semi-barbarous Asia, princesses who have never been seen by men, other than those of their own family, or ever spoken with them unless from behind a curtain, have as regents, during the minority of

---

* An excellent passage on this part of the subject, from one of Sydney Smith's contributions to the 'Edinburgh Review,' we must not refrain from quoting:—
"A great deal has been said of the original difference of capacity between men and women, as if women were more quick and men more judicious—as if women were more remarkable for delicacy of association, and men for stronger powers of attention. All this, we confess, appears to us very fanciful. That there is a difference in the understandings of the men and the women we every day meet with, everybody, we suppose, must perceive; but there is none surely which may not be accounted for by the difference of circumstances in which they have been placed, without referring to any conjectural difference of original conformation of mind. As long as boys and girls run about in the dirt, and trundle hoops together, they are both precisely alike. If you catch up one-half of these creatures, and train them to a particular set of actions and opinions, and the other half to a perfectly opposite set, of course their understandings will differ, as one or the other sort of occupations has called this or that talent into action. There is surely no occasion to go into any deeper or more abstruse reasoning, in order to explain so very simple a phenomenon."—*Sydney Smith's Works*, vol. i. p. 200.

their sons, exhibited many of the most brilliant examples of just and vigorous administration. In the middle ages, when the distance between the upper and lower ranks was greater than even between women and men, and the women of the privileged class, however subject to tyranny from the men of the same class, were at a less distance below them than any one else, and often in their absence represented them in their functions of authority—numbers of heroic châtelaines, like Jeanne de Montfort, or the great Countess of Derby as late even as the time of Charles I., distinguished themselves not only by their political but their military capacity. In the centuries immediately before and after the Reformation, ladies of royal houses, as diplomatists, as governors of provinces, or as the confidential advisers of kings, equalled the first statesmen of their time: and the treaty of Cambray, which gave peace to Europe, was negotiated in conferences where no other person was present, by the aunt of the Emperor Charles the Fifth, and the mother of Francis the First.

Concerning the fitness, then, of women for politics, there can be no question: but the dispute is more likely to turn upon the fitness of politics for women. When the reasons alleged for excluding women from active life in all its higher departments, are stripped of their garb of declamatory phrases, and reduced to the simple expression of a meaning, they seem to be mainly three: the incompatibility of active life with maternity, and with the cares of a household; secondly, its alleged hardening effect on the character; and thirdly, the inexpediency of making an addition to the already excessive pressure of competition in every kind of professional or lucrative employment.

The first, the maternity argument, is usually laid most stress upon: although (it needs hardly be said) this reason, if it be one, can apply only to mothers. It is neither necessary nor just to make imperative on women that they should be either mothers or nothing; or that if they had been mothers once, they shall be nothing else during the whole remainder of their lives. Neither women nor men need any law to exclude them from an occupation, if they have undertaken another which is incompatible with it. No one proposes to exclude the male sex from Parliament because a man may be a soldier or sailor in active service, or a merchant whose business requires all his time and energies. Nine-tenths of the occupations of men exclude them *de facto* from public life, as effectually as if they were excluded by law; but that is no reason for making laws to exclude even the nine-tenths, much less the remaining tenth. The reason of the case is the same for women as for men. There is no need to make provision by law that a woman shall not carry on the active details of a household, or of the education of children, and at the same time practise a profession or be elected to parliament. Where incompatibility is real, it will take care of itself: but there is gross injustice in making the incompatibility a pretence for the exclusion of those in whose case it does not exist. And these, if they were free to choose, would be a very large proportion. The maternity argument deserts its supporters in the case of single women, a large and increasing class of the population; a fact which, it is not irrelevant to remark, by tending to diminish the excessive competition of numbers, is calculated to assist greatly the prosperity of all. There is no inherent reason or necessity that all women should voluntarily choose to devote their lives to one animal function and its consequences. Numbers of women are wives and mothers only because there is no other career open to them, no other occupation for their feelings or their activities. Every improvement in their education, and enlargement of their faculties—everything which renders them more qualified for any other mode of life, increases the number of those to whom it is an injury and an oppression to be denied the choice. To say that women must be excluded from active life because maternity disqualifies them for it, is in fact to say, that every other career should be forbidden them in order that maternity may be their only resource.

But secondly, it is urged, that to give the same freedom of occupation to women as to men, would be an injurious addition to the crowd of competitors, by whom the avenues to almost all kinds of employment are choked up, and its remuneration depressed. This argument, it is to be observed, does not reach the political question. It gives no excuse for withholding from women the rights of citizenship. The suffrage, the jury-box, admission to the legislature and to office, it does not touch. It bears only on the industrial branch of the subject. Allowing it, then, in an economical point of view, its full force; assuming that to lay open to women the employments now monopolized by men, would tend, like the breaking down of other monopolies, to lower the rate of remuneration in those employments,—let us consider what is the amount of this evil consequence, and what the compensation for it. The worst ever asserted, much worse than is at all likely to be realized, is that if women competed with men, a man and a woman could not together earn more than is now earned by the man alone. Let us make this supposition, the most unfavourable supposition possible: the joint income of the two would be the same as before, while the woman would be raised from the position of a servant to that of a partner. Even if every woman, as matters now stand, had a claim on some man for support, how infinitely preferable is it that part of the income should be of the woman's earning, even if the aggregate sum were but little increased by it, rather than that she should be compelled to stand aside in order that men may be the sole earners, and the sole dispensers of what is earned! Even under the present laws respecting the property of women,* a woman who contributes materially to the support of the family, cannot be treated in the same contemptuously tyrannical manner as one who, however she may toil as a domestic drudge, is a dependant on the man for subsistence. As for the depression of wages by increase of competition, remedies will be found for it in time. Palliatives might be applied immediately; for in-

* The truly horrible effects of the present state of the law among the lowest of the working population, is exhibited in those cases of hideous maltreatment of their wives by working men, with which every newspaper, every police report, teems. Wretches unfit to have the smallest authority over any living thing, have a helpless woman for their household slave. These excesses could not exist, if women both earned, and had the right to possess, a part of the income of the family.

stance, a more rigid exclusion of children from industrial employment, during the years in which they ought to be working only to strengthen their bodies and minds for after-life. Children are *necessarily* dependent, and under the power of others; and their labour, being not for themselves but for the gain of their parents, is a proper subject for legislative regulation. With respect to the future, we neither believe that improvident multiplication, and the consequent excessive difficulty of gaining a subsistence, will eternally continue, nor that the division of mankind into capitalists and hired labourers, and the regulation of the reward of labourers mainly by demand and supply, will be for ever, or even much longer, the rule of the world. But so long as competition is the general law of human life, it is tyranny to shut out one-half of the competitors. All who have attained the age of self-government, have an equal claim to be permitted to sell whatever kind of useful labour they are capable of, for the price which it will bring.

The third objection to the admission of women to political or professional life, its alleged hardening tendency, belongs to an age now past, and is scarcely to be comprehended by people of the present time. There are still, however, persons who say that the world and its avocations render men selfish and unfeeling; that the struggles, rivalries and collisions of business and of politics make them harsh and unamiable; that if half the species must unavoidably be given up to these things, it is the more necessary that the other half should be kept free from them; that to preserve women from the bad influences of the world, is the only chance of preventing men from being wholly given up to them.

There would have been plausibility in this argument when the world was still in the age of violence, when life was full of physical conflict, and every man had to redress his injuries or those of others, by the sword or by the strength of his arm. Women, like priests, by being exempted from such responsibilities, and from some part of the accompanying dangers, may have been enabled to exercise a beneficial influence. But in the present condition of human life, we do not know where those hardening influences are to be found, to which men are subject and from which women are at present exempt. Individuals nowadays are seldom called upon to fight hand to hand, even with peaceful weapons; personal enmities and rivalities count for little in worldly transactions; the general pressure of circumstances, not the adverse will of individuals, is the obstacle men now have to make head against. That pressure, when excessive, breaks the spirit, and cramps and sours the feelings, but not less of women than of men, since they suffer certainly not less from its evils. There are still quarrels and dislikes, but the sources of them are changed. The feudal chief once found his bitterest enemy in his powerful neighbour, the minister or courtier in his rival for place: but opposition of interest in active life, as a cause of personal animosity, is out of date; the enmities of the present day arise not from great things but small, from what people say of one another, more than from what they do; and if there are hatred, malice, and all uncharitableness, they are to be found among women fully as much as among men. In the present state of civilization, the notion of guarding women from the hardening influences of the world, could only be realized by secluding them from society altogether. The common duties of common life, as at present constituted, are incompatible with any other softness in women than weakness. Surely weak minds in weak bodies must ere long cease to be even supposed to be either attractive or amiable.

But, in truth, none of these arguments and considerations touch the foundations of the subject. The real question is, whether it is right and expedient that one-half of the human race should pass through life in a state of forced subordination to the other half. If the best state of human society is that of being divided into two parts, one consisting of persons with a will and a substantive existence, the other of humble companions to these persons, attached, each of them to one, for the purpose of bringing up *his* children, and making *his* home pleasant to him; if this is the place assigned to women, it is but kindness to educate them for this; to make them believe that the greatest good fortune which can befall them, is to be chosen by some man for this purpose; and that every other career which the world deems happy or honourable, is closed to them by the law, not of social institutions, but of nature and destiny.

When, however, we ask why the existence of one-half the species should be merely ancillary to that of the other—why each woman should be a mere appendage to a man, allowed to have no interests of her own, that there may be nothing to compete in her mind with his interests and his pleasure,—the only reason which can be given is, that men like it. It is agreeable to them that men should live for their own sake, women for the sake of men: and the qualities and conduct in subjects which are agreeable to rulers, they succeed for a long time in making the subjects themselves consider as their appropriate virtues. Helvetius has met with much obloquy for asserting, that persons usually mean by virtues the qualities which are useful or convenient to themselves. How truly this is said of mankind in general, and how wonderfully the ideas of virtue set afloat by the powerful, are caught and imbibed by those under their dominion, is exemplified by the manner in which the world were once persuaded that the supreme virtue of subjects was loyalty to kings, and are still persuaded that the paramount virtue of womanhood is loyalty to man. Under a nominal recognition of a moral code common to both, in practice self-will and self-assertion form the type of what are designated as manly virtues, while abnegation of self, patience, resignation, and submission to power, unless when resistance is commanded by other interests than their own, have been stamped by general consent as pre-eminently the duties and graces required of women,—the meaning being merely, that power makes itself the centre of moral obligation, and that a man likes to have his own will, but does not like that his domestic companion should have a will different from his.

We are far from pretending that in modern and civilized times, no reciprocity of obligation is acknowledged on the part of the stronger. Such an assertion would be very wide of the truth. But even the reciprocity, which has disarmed tyranny at least in the higher and middle classes, of its most revolting features, yet when combined with the original evil of the dependent condition of women, has introduced in its turn serious evils.

In the beginning, and amongst tribes which are still in a primitive condition, women were and are the slaves of men for purposes of toil. All the hard bodily labour devolves on them. The Australian savage is idle, while women painfully dig up the roots on which he lives. An American Indian, when he has killed a deer, leaves it, and sends a woman to carry it home. In a state somewhat more advanced, as in Asia, women were and are the slaves of men for the purposes of sensuality. In Europe there early succeeded a third and milder dominion, secured not by blows, nor by locks and bars, but by sedulous inculcation on the mind; feelings also of kindness, and ideas of duty, such as a superior owes to inferiors under his protection, become more and more involved in the relation. But it did not for many ages become a relation of companionship, even between unequals; the lives of the two persons were apart. The wife was part of the furniture of home, of the resting-place to which the man returned from business or pleasure. His occupations were, as they still are, among men; his pleasures and excitements also were, for the most part, among men—among his equals. He was a patriarch and a despot within four walls, and irresponsible power had its effect, greater or less according to his disposition, in rendering him domineering, exacting, self-worshipping, when not capriciously or brutally tyrannical. But if the moral part of his nature suffered, it was not necessarily so, in the same degree, with the intellectual or the active portion. He might have as much vigour of mind and energy of character as his nature enabled him, and as the circumstances of his times allowed. He might write the 'Paradise Lost,' or win the battle of Marengo. This was the condition of the Greeks and Romans, and of the moderns until a recent date. Their relations with their domestic subordinates occupied a mere corner, though a cherished one, of their lives. Their education as men, the formation of their character and faculties, depended mainly on a different class of influences.

It is otherwise now. The progress of improvement has imposed on all possessors of power, and of domestic power among the rest, an increased and increasing sense of correlative obligation. No man now thinks that his wife has no claim upon his actions, but such as he may accord to her. All men of any conscience believe that their duty to their wives is one of the most binding of their obligations. Nor is it supposed to consist solely in protection, which, in the present state of civilization, women have almost ceased to need: it involves care for their happiness and consideration of their wishes, with a not unfrequent sacrifice of their own to them. The power of husbands has reached the stage which the power of kings had arrived at, when opinion did not yet question the rightfulness of arbitrary power, but in theory, and to a certain extent in practice, condemned the selfish use of it. This improvement in the moral sentiments of mankind, and increased sense of the consideration due by every man to those who had no one but himself to look to, has tended to make home more and more the centre of interest, and domestic circumstances and society a larger and larger part of life, and of its pursuits and pleasures. The tendency has been strengthened by the changes of tastes and manners which have so remarkably distinguished the last two or three generations. In days not far distant, men found their excitement and filled up their time in violent bodily exercises, noisy merriment, and intemperance. They have now, in all but the very poorest classes, lost their inclination for these things, and for the coarser pleasures generally; they have now scarcely any tastes but those which they have in common with women, and, for the first time in the world, men and women are really companions. A most beneficial change, if the companionship were between equals; but being between unequals, it produces, what good observers have noticed, though without perceiving its cause, a progressive deterioration among men in what had hitherto been considered the masculine excellences. Those who are so careful that women should not become men, do not see that men are becoming what they have decided that women should be—are falling into the feebleness which they have so long cultivated in their companions. Those who are associated in their lives, tend to become assimilated in character. In the present closeness of association between the sexes, men cannot retain manliness unless women acquire it.

There is hardly any situation more unfavourable to the maintenance of elevation of character or force of intellect, than to live in the society, and seek by preference the sympathy of inferiors in mental endowments. Why is it that we constantly see in life so much of intellectual and moral promise followed by such inadequate performance, but because the aspirant has compared himself only with those below himself, and has not sought improvement or stimulus from measuring himself with his equals or superiors? In the present state of social life, this is becoming the general condition of men. They care less and less for any sympathies, and are less and less under any personal influences, but those of the domestic roof. Not to be misunderstood, it is necessary that we should distinctly disclaim the belief, that women are even now inferior in intellect to men. There are women who are the equals in intellect of any men who ever lived: and comparing ordinary women with ordinary men, the varied though petty details which compose the occupation of most women, call forth probably as much of mental ability as the uniform routine of the pursuits which are the habitual occupation of a large majority of men. It is from nothing in the faculties themselves, but from the petty subjects and interests on which alone they are exercised, that the companionship of women, such as their present circumstances make them, so often exercises a dissolvent influence on high faculties and aspirations in men. If one of the two has no knowledge and no care about the great ideas and purposes which dignify life, or about any of its practical concerns save personal interests and personal vanities, her conscious, and still more her unconscious influence, will, except in rare cases, reduce to a secondary place in his mind, if not entirely extinguish, those interests which she cannot or does not share.

Our argument here brings us into collision with what may be termed the moderate reformers of the education of women; a sort of persons who cross the path of improvement on all great questions; those who would maintain the old bad principles, mitigating their consequences. These say that women should be, not slaves nor servants, but companions; and educated for that office: (they do not say that men should be educated to be the companions of women). But since uncultivated women are not suitable companions for cultivated men, and a man who feels interest in things above and beyond the family circle wishes that his companion should sympathize with him in that interest,—they therefore say, let women improve their understanding and taste, acquire general knowledge, cultivate poetry, art, even coquet with science, and some stretch their liberality so far as to say, inform themselves on politics; not as pursuits, but sufficiently to feel an interest in the subjects, and to be capable of holding a conversation on them with the husband, or at least of understanding and imbibing his wisdom. Very agreeable to him, no doubt, but unfortunately the reverse of improving. It is from having intellectual communion only with those to whom they can lay down the law, that so few men continue to advance in wisdom beyond the first stages. The most eminent men cease to improve, if they associate only with disciples. When they have overtopped those who immediately surround them, if they wish for further growth, they must seek for others of their own stature to consort with. The mental companionship which is improving, is communion between active minds, not mere contact between an active mind and a passive. This inestimable advantage is even now enjoyed, when a strong-minded man and a strong-minded woman are, by a rare chance, united: and would be had far oftener, if education took the same pains to form strong-minded women which it takes to prevent them from being formed. But this supposes other than mere *dilettante* instruction, given as an elegant amusement or agreeable accomplishment, not as a power to be used. Mental cultivation adapted for show and not for use, which makes pigmies of men, is the only kind given or proposed to be given to women by the present reformers of their education. What makes intelligent beings is the power of thought: the stimuli which call forth that power are the interest and dignity of thought itself, and a field for its practical application. Both motives are cut off from those who are told from infancy that thought, and all its greater applications, are other people's business, while theirs is to make themselves agreeable to other people. High mental powers in women will be but an exceptional accident, until every career is open to them, and until they, as well as men, are educated for themselves and for the world—not one sex for the other.

In what we have said on the effect of the inferior position of women, combined with the present constitution of married life, we have thus far had in view only the most favourable cases, those in which there is some real approach to that union and blending of characters and of lives, which the theory of the relation contemplates as its ideal standard. But if we look to the great majority of cases, the effect of women's legal inferiority on the character both of women and of men must be painted in far darker colours. We do not speak here of the grosser brutalities, nor of the man's power to seize on the woman's earnings, or compel her to live with him against her will. We do not address ourselves to any one who requires to have it proved that these things should be remedied. We suppose average cases, in which there is neither complete union nor complete disunion of feelings and of character; and we affirm that in such cases the influence of the dependence on the woman's side, is demoralizing to the character of both.

The common opinion is, that whatever may be the case with the intellectual, the moral influence of women over men is almost always salutary. It is, we are often told, the great counteractive of selfishness. However the case may be as to personal influence, the influence of the position tends eminently to promote selfishness. The most insignificant of men, the man who can obtain influence or consideration nowhere else, finds one place where he is chief and head. There is one person, often greatly his superior in understanding, who is obliged to consult him, and whom he is not obliged to consult. He is judge, magistrate, ruler, over their joint concerns; arbiter of all differences between them. The justice or conscience to which her appeal must be made, is his justice and conscience: it is his to hold the balance and adjust the scales between his own claims or wishes and those of another. His is now the only tribunal, in civilized life, in which the same person is judge and party. A generous mind, such a situation, makes the balance incline against its own side, and gives the other not less, but more, than a fair equality; and thus the weaker side may be enabled to turn the very fact of dependence into an instrument of power, and, in default of justice, take an ungenerous advantage of generosity,—rendering the unjust power, to those who make an unselfish use of it, a torment and a burthen. But how is it when average men are invested with this power, without reciprocity and without responsibility? Give such a man the idea that he is first in law and in opinion—that to will is his part, and hers to submit; it is absurd to suppose that this idea merely glides over his mind, without sinking into it, or having any effect on his feelings and practice. The propensity to make himself the first object of consideration, and others at most the second, is not so rare as to be wanting where everything seems purposely arranged for permitting its indulgence. If there is any self-will in the man, he becomes either the conscious or unconscious despot of his household. The wife, indeed, often succeeds in gaining her objects, but it is by some of the many various forms of indirectness and management.

Thus the position is corrupting equally to both; in the one it produces the vices of power, in the other those of artifice. Women, in their present physical and moral state, having stronger impulses, would naturally be franker and more direct than men; yet all the old saws and traditions represent them as artful and dissembling. Why? Because their only way to their objects is by indirect paths. In all countries where women have strong wishes and active minds, this consequence is inevitable: and if it is less conspicuous in England than in some other places, it is because Englishwomen, saving occasional exceptions, have ceased to have either strong wishes or active minds.

We are not now speaking of cases in which there is anything deserving the name of strong affection on both sides. That, where it exists, is too powerful a principle not to modify greatly the bad influences of the situation; it seldom, however, destroys them entirely. Much oftener the bad influences are too strong for the affection, and destroy it. The highest order of durable and happy attachments would be a hundred times more frequent than they are, if the affection which the two sexes sought from one another were that genuine friendship, which only exists between equals in privileges as in faculties. But with regard to what is commonly called affection in married life—the habitual and almost mechanical feeling of kindliness, and pleasure in each other's society, which generally grows up between persons who constantly live together, unless there is actual dislike—there is nothing in this to contradict or qualify the mischievous influence of the unequal relation. Such feelings often exist between a sultan and his favourites, between a master and his servants; they are merely examples of the pliability of human nature, which accommodates itself in some degree even to the worst circumstances, and the commonest natures always the most easily.

With respect to the influence personally exercised by women over men, it, no doubt, renders them less harsh and brutal; in ruder times, it was often the only softening influence to which they were accessible. But the assertion, that the wife's influence renders the man less selfish, contains, as things now are, fully as much error as truth. Selfishness towards the wife herself, and towards those in whom she is interested, the children, though favoured by their dependence, the wife's influence, no doubt, tends to counteract. But the general effect on him of her character, so long as her interests are concentrated in the family, tends but to substitute for individual selfishness a family selfishness, wearing an amiable guise, and putting on the mask of duty. How rarely is the wife's influence on the side of public virtue : how rarely does it do otherwise than discourage any effort of principle by which the private interests or worldly vanities of the family can be expected to suffer! Public spirit, sense of duty towards the public good, is of all virtues, as women are now educated and situated, the most rarely to be found among them; they have seldom even, what in men is often a partial substitute for public spirit, a sense of personal honour connected with any public duty. Many a man, whom no money or personal flattery would have bought, has bartered his political opinions against titles or invitations to his wife; and a still greater number are made mere hunters after the puerile vanities of society, because their wives value them. As for opinions, in Catholic countries the wife's influence is another name for that of the priest; he gives her, in the hopes and emotions connected with a future life, a consolation for the sufferings and disappointments which are her ordinary lot in this. Elsewhere, her weight is thrown into the scale either of the most commonplace or of the most outwardly prosperous opinions; either those by which censure will be escaped, or by which worldly advancement is likeliest to be procured. In England, the wife's influence is usually on the illiberal and anti-popular side: this is generally the gaining side for personal interest and vanity; and what to her is the democracy or liberalism in which she has no part—which leaves her the Pariah it found her? The man himself, when he marries, usually declines into Conservatism, begins to sympathize with the holders of power more than with its victims, and thinks it his part to be on the side of authority. As to mental progress, except those vulgarer attainments by which vanity or ambition are promoted, there is generally an end to them in a man who marries a woman mentally his inferior; unless, indeed, he is unhappy in marriage, or becomes indifferent. From a man of twenty-five or thirty, after he is married, an experienced observer seldom expects any further progress in mind or feelings. It is rare that the progress already made is maintained. Any spark of the *mens divinior* which might otherwise have spread and become a flame, seldom survives for any length of time unextinguished. For a mind which learns to be satisfied with what it already is—which does not incessantly look forward to a degree of improvement not yet reached—becomes relaxed, self-indulgent, and loses the spring and the tension which maintain it even at the point already attained. And there is no fact in human nature to which experience bears more invariable testimony than to this—that all social or sympathetic influences which do not raise up, pull down; if they do not tend to stimulate and exalt the mind, they tend to vulgarize it.

For the interest, therefore, not only of women but of men, and of human improvement in the widest sense, the emancipation of women, which the modern world often boasts of having effected, and for which credit is sometimes given to civilization, and sometimes to Christianity, cannot stop where it is. If it were either necessary or just that one portion of mankind should remain mentally and spiritually only half developed, the development of the other portion ought to have been made, as far as possible, independent of their influence. Instead of this, they have become the most intimate, and it may now be said, the only intimate associates of those to whom yet they are sedulously kept inferior; and have been raised just high enough to drag the others down to themselves.

We have left behind a host of vulgar objections, either as not worthy of an answer, or as answered by the general course of our remarks. A few words, however, must be said on one plea, which in England is made much use of for giving an unselfish air to the upholding of selfish privileges, and which, with unobserving, unreflecting people, passes for much more than it is worth. Women, it is said, do not desire—do not seek, what is called their emancipation. On the contrary, they generally disown such claims when made in their behalf, and fall with *acharnement* upon any one of themselves who identifies herself with their common cause.

Supposing the fact to be true in the fullest extent ever asserted, if it proves that European women ought to remain as they are, it proves exactly the same with respect to Asiatic women; for they too, instead of murmuring at their seclusion, and at the restraint imposed upon them, pride themselves on it, and are astonished at the effrontery of women who receive visits from male acquaintances, and are seen in the streets unveiled. Habits of submission make men as well as women servile-minded. The vast population of Asia do not desire or value, probably would not accept, political liberty, nor the savages of the forest, civilization; which does not prove that either of those things is undesirable for them, or that they will not, at some future time, enjoy it. Custom hardens human beings to any kind of degradation, by deadening the part of their nature which would resist it. And the case of women is, in this respect, even a peculiar one, for no other inferior caste that we have heard of, have been taught to regard their degradation as their honour. The argument, however, implies a secret consciousness that the alleged preference of women for their dependent state is merely apparent, and arises from their being allowed no choice; for if the preference be natural, there can be no necessity for enforcing it by law. To make laws compelling people to follow their inclination, has not hitherto been thought necessary by any legislator. The plea that women do not desire any change, is the same that has been urged, times out of mind, against the proposal of abolishing any social evil,—" There is no complaint;" which is generally not true, and when true, only so because there is not that hope of success, without which complaint seldom makes itself audible to unwilling ears. How does the objector know that women do not desire equality and freedom? He never knew a woman who did not, or would not, desire it for herself individually. It would be very simple to suppose, that if they do desire it they will say so. Their position is like that of the tenants or labourers who vote against their own political interests to please their landlords or employers; with the unique addition, that submission is inculcated on them from childhood, as the peculiar attraction and grace of their character. They are taught to think, that to repel actively even an admitted injustice done to themselves, is somewhat unfeminine, and had better be left to some male friend or protector. To be accused of rebelling against anything which admits of being called an ordinance of society, they are taught to regard as an imputation of a serious offence, to say the least, against the proprieties of their sex. It requires unusual moral courage as well as disinterestedness in a woman, to express opinions favourable to women's enfranchisement, until, at least, there is some prospect of obtaining it. The comfort of her individual life, and her social consideration, usually depend on the goodwill of those who hold the undue power; and to possessors of power any complaint, however bitter, of the misuse of it, is a less flagrant act of insubordination than to protest against the power itself. The professions of women in this matter remind us of the State offenders of old, who, on the point of execution, used to protest their love and devotion to the sovereign by whose unjust mandate they suffered. Griselda herself might be matched from the speeches put by Shakespeare into the mouths of male victims of kingly caprice and tyranny: the Duke of Buckingham, for example, in 'Henry the Eighth,' and even Wolsey. The literary class of women, especially in England, are ostentatious in disclaiming the desire for equality or citizenship, and proclaiming their complete satisfaction with the place which society assigns to them,—exercising in this, as in many other respects, a most noxious influence over the feelings and opinions of men, who unsuspectingly accept the servilities of toadyism as concessions to the force of truth, not considering that it is the personal interest of these women to profess whatever opinions they expect will be agreeable to men. It is not among men of talent, sprung from the people, and patronized and flattered by the aristocracy, that we look for the leaders of a democratic movement. Successful literary women are just as unlikely to prefer the cause of women to their own social consideration. They depend on men's opinion for their literary as well as for their feminine successes; and such is their bad opinion of men, that they believe there is not more than one in ten thousand who does not dislike and fear strength, sincerity, or high spirit in a woman. They are therefore anxious to earn pardon and toleration for whatever of these qualities their writings may exhibit on other subjects, by a studied display of submission on this, that they may give no occasion for vulgar men to say (what nothing will prevent vulgar men from saying), that learning makes women unfeminine, and that literary ladies are likely to be bad wives.

But enough of this; especially as the fact which affords the occasion for this paper, makes it impossible any longer to assert the universal acquiescence of women (saving individual exceptions) in their dependent condition. In the United States at least, there are women, seemingly numerous, and now organized for action on the public mind, who demand equality in the fullest acceptation of the word, and demand it by a straightforward appeal to men's sense of justice, not plead for it with a timid deprecation of their displeasure.

Like other popular movements, however, this may be seriously retarded by the blunders of its adherents. Tried by the ordinary standard of public meetings, the speeches at the Convention are remarkable for the preponderance of the rational over the declamatory element; but there are some exceptions; and things to which it is impossible to attach any rational meaning, have found their way into the resolutions. Thus, the resolution which sets forth the claims made in behalf of women, after claiming equality in education, in industrial pursuits, and in political rights, enumerates as a fourth head of demand something under the name of "social and spiritual union," and "a medium of expressing the highest moral and spiritual views of justice," with other similar verbiage, serving only to mar the simplicity and rationality of the other demands. What is wanted for women is equal rights, equal admission to all social privileges; not a position apart, a sort of sentimental priesthood. To this, the only just and rational principle, both the resolutions and the speeches, for the most part, adhere. They contain so little which is akin to the nonsensical paragraph in question, that we suspect it not to be the work of the same hands as most of the other resolutions. The strength of the cause lies in the support of those who are influenced by reason and principle; and to attempt to recommend it by sentimentalities, absurd in reason and inconsistent with the principle on which the movement is founded, is to place a good cause on a level with a bad one.

There are indications that the example of America will be followed on this side of the Atlantic; and the first step has been taken in that part of England where every serious movement in the direction of political progress has its commencement—the manufacturing districts of the North. On the 13th of February, 1851, a petition of women, agreed to by a public meeting at Sheffield, and claiming the elective franchise, was presented to the House of Lords by the Earl of Carlisle.

THE END.

PRINTED BY J. E. TAYLOR AND CO.,
LITTLE QUEEN STREET, LINCOLN'S INN FIELDS.

THE EXAMINER has appeared in an altered shape since the commencement of last year. Instead of the sixteen pages to which the weekly issue had previously been limited, twenty-four smaller pages are now given, with the occasional addition of four or eight; the intention being that, exclusive of the space occupied by advertisements, an average of twenty pages of original matter shall be furnished each week.

Change of outward form, however, is only a small part of the change that has been undertaken. "The main objects of THE EXAMINER newspaper," said LEIGH HUNT of the work which he and his brother JOHN HUNT commenced in 1808, "were to assist in producing reform in Parliament, liberality of opinion in general, especially freedom from superstition, and a fusion of literary tastes into all subjects whatever." Great advances have been made in political, social, and literary progress during the four-and-sixty years which the lifetime of THE EXAMINER already covers, and many good reforms, in which LEIGH HUNT. ALBANY FONBLANQUE, and their associates were pioneers, have been achieved; but these reforms have only prepared the way for others yet to be effected. THE EXAMINER, in accordance with its original principles and traditions, attempts to do as much useful service to the cause of progress now as it has done in former years. It strives honestly and heartily to aid its readers in forming sound opinions concerning the important events of the day, and in drawing therefrom such conclusions as may promote wise thought and fearless action towards the removal of errors and abuses from which the world still suffers, and towards the development of views that are necessary to the increased well being of all classes of society. As many independent thinkers give expression to their opinions in the pages of THE EXAMINER, and none of em claim to be infallible, no attempt is made to obtain com agreement in the views put forward; but in the fundamenta. nciples which prompt them there is no variation.

THE EXAMINER is published on Saturdays, in time for the early morning mails, or for delivery with the daily papers. PRICE THREEPENCE.

Subscribers may have their copies sent, post free, direct from the Office, No. 9 Wellington-street, Strand, on payment in advance of 3s. 9d. a quarter.

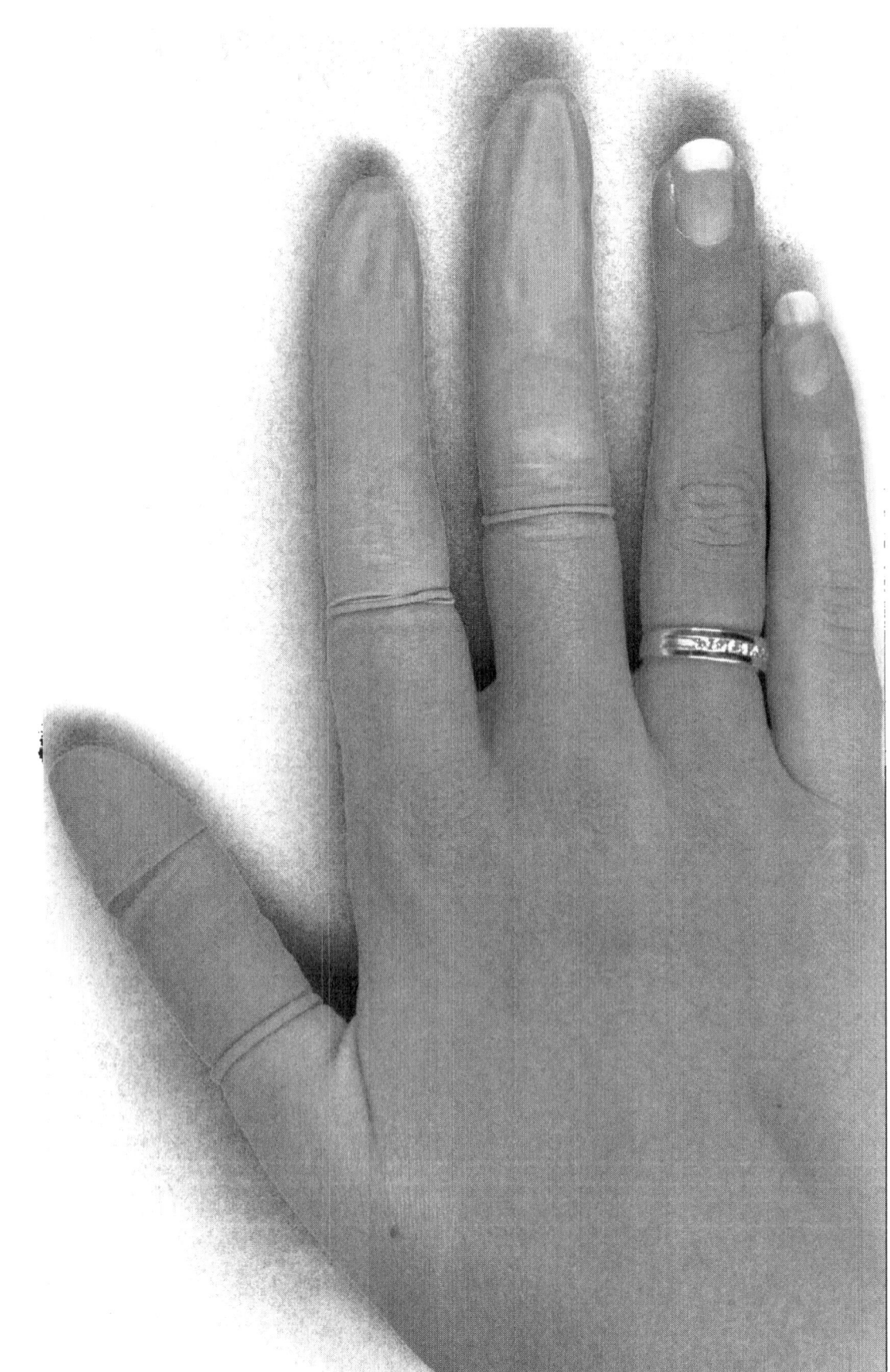

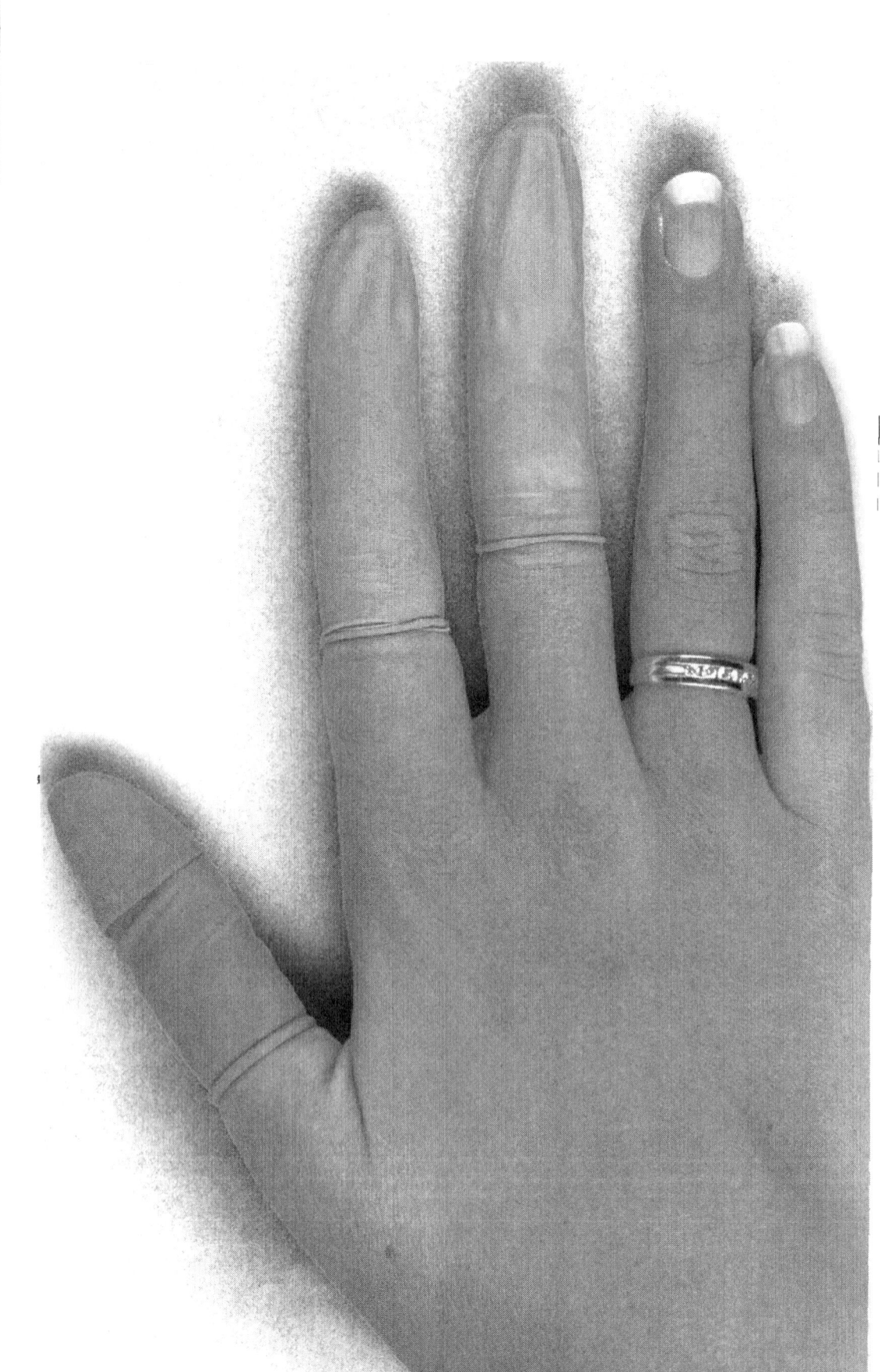

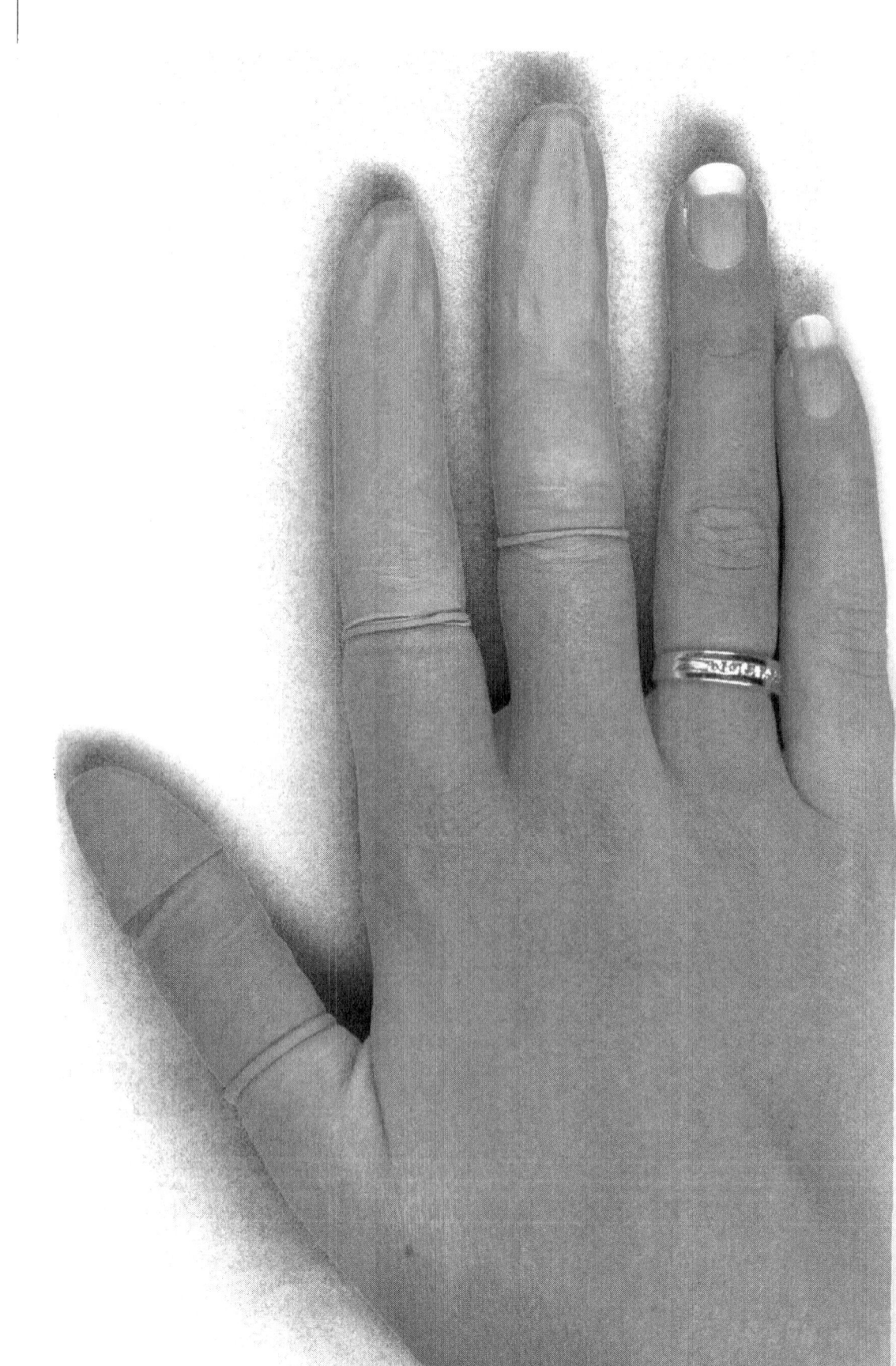

Lightning Source UK Ltd.
Milton Keynes UK
UKOW07f0911190715

255370UK00007B/94/P